Cobden Club

Lord Farrer on the free trade question

Cobden Club

Lord Farrer on the free trade question

ISBN/EAN: 9783337277734

Printed in Europe, USA, Canada, Australia, Japan

Cover: Foto ©Suzi / pixelio.de

More available books at **www.hansebooks.com**

LORD FARRER

ON

The Free Trade Question.

MR. J. W. PROBYN AND MR. I. S. LEADAM

ON THE

WORK OF THE COBDEN CLUB.

THE COBDEN CLUB AND PRISON-MADE GOODS.

THE ANNUAL GENERAL MEETING

OF

THE COBDEN CLUB, 1895,

WITH

THE COMMITTEE'S REPORT

AND SPEECHES BY

LORD FARRER, Mr. J. W. PROBYN, Mr. I. S LEADAM,
Mr. PROVAND, M.P.,
SIR WILFRID LAWSON, BART., M.P., Mr. THOMAS HANBURY,
Mr. GEORGE LOUGH, M.P., M. EDOUARD SEVE,
Mr. GEORGE COLE, Mr. G. J. HOLYOAKE, Mr. SOPER,
Mr. MARTIN WOOD, THE CHAIRMAN (Mr. T. B. POTTER),
AND OTHERS.

PRINTED FOR THE COBDEN CLUB,
1895.

ANNUAL MEETING OF THE COBDEN CLUB,

AUGUST 17th, 1895,

MR. THOMAS BAYLEY POTTER

IN THE CHAIR.

The twenty-ninth annual general meeting of the Cobden Club was held in the Conference Room at the National Liberal Club, London, on Saturday, the 17th of August. Mr. Thomas Bayley Potter, the honorary secretary to the Club and president of the Committee, occupied the chair, and there were present Lord Farrer, Sir Wilfrid Lawson, Bart., M.P., the Right Hon. Sir A. D. Hayter, Bart., the Right Hon. C. Seale-Hayne, M.P., Mr. F. A. Channing, M.P., Mr. A. D. Provand, M.P., Mr. J. W. Probyn (hon treasurer), Mrs. T. Fisher Unwin (daughter of Mr. Cobden), Mr. Thomas Lough, M.P., Mr. James Bruyn Andrews (U.S. America), Mr. I. S. Leadam, Mr. T. Fisher Unwin, Mr. Dadabhai Naoroji (India), M. Chedoille Mijatovich (Servian Minister), Mr. Thomas Hanbury, M. Edouard Sève (Belgian Consul General), Mr. Thomas E. Thorley, Mr. M. Macfie, Mr. George Jacob Holyoake, Mr. H. R. Fox Bourne, Mr. G. Blomquist (Sweden), Dr. A. Brown, Mr. Thomas Blandford, Mr. Edward Goadby, Mr. Harold Hamel Smith, Mr. George Cole (Canterbury), Mr. W. B. J. Williams, Mr. William J. Ford, Mr. F. L. Soper, Mr. Martin Wood, Mr. G. J. Knight, Mr. Richard Gowing (secretary), etc.

MR. T. B. POTTER.

The CHAIRMAN said: Gentlemen, with your permission I propose to alter the order of our proceedings, inasmuch as our friend, Lord Farrer, is obliged to leave us early. I shall therefore call upon him to address you before Mr. Gowing reads the annual report.

A

LORD FARRER.

Lord FARRER: Gentlemen, I am extremely indebted to Mr. Potter and to you for allowing me to come before you at the beginning of your meeting. An engagement has been made for me which I cannot well put off, and I must needs get away early. I am well acquainted with the report of the Committee, and the remarks that I have to make will, I trust, be apposite to it.

THE GENERAL POSITION OF FREE TRADE ABROAD.

As regards the general position of matters in relation to the subject in which we are most nearly interested I am glad to be able to say that it is more favourable than any of us a short time ago had a right to expect. On the whole the position is very favourable. There is an obvious movement in the Australian colonies, some of which have been great centres of Protection, betokening a reaction in the direction of Free Trade. They have tried Protection as a remedy for trade depression, but it has availed them nothing; and I trust that, sooner or later, they will, in some way or another, come round to Free Trade. I trust that before long we shall have not only something approaching to Free Trade between the different Australian colonies, but something like Free Trade between those colonies and the rest of the British Empire, and between those colonies and foreign countries. It is a little difficult and delicate to speak about the United States—the country upon which the commercial welfare of the world so largely depends—but so far as one can judge, the prospect there is promising if they can but get rid of their currency difficulties. But into that question I will not enter. There is, apparently, before the United States a period of great prosperity, and if with a period of prosperity they find that the modifications that were made in the Mc.Kinley tariff have brought them no disadvantage, but rather substantial advantages, that circumstance will probably create an inclination to extend the principle of Free Trade in other directions.

AT HOME.

Speaking modestly on these two subjects, but still hopefully, I turn to domestic matters. I think that on several points I can speak more hopefully than in 1891, 1892, and again in 1893. In those years we were confronted with many dangers. One of them was the danger arising from Lord Salisbury's statement that he wished to have Protective duties put upon foreign manufactures in order the better to fight foreign tariffs. But we have heard very little of that statement lately; and I expect that as Lord Salisbury is now himself in a responsible position, we shall hear still less about it. His Lordship is now strong enough to set aside those members of his own party who would move him in a false direction. At the same time I would strongly advise all Free Traders to keep a careful watch on his doings, and not only on Lord Salisbury but on the doings of the Foreign Office. It is a very tempting thing for the permanent officials of the Foreign Office and for ambassadors, when asked to make commercial treaties on behalf of this country, to say "We have no weapons at our command to give effect to the principle of Free Trade. Have some duties that you can take off, and then we shall be able to make better bargains." We all know the fallacy of that view, but it is one which is very likely to prevail at the Foreign Office; and, therefore, I say "Beware of the Foreign Office!"

THE TRADES UNIONS AND FREE TRADE.

The second danger, of which I have spoken on a former occasion, is the danger lest Trades Unions, which have been in former times themselves oppressed, should now seek to tyrannise and to control the means of production. If they attempt to do that—and some of their leaders certainly have a strong desire to do it—and if they find they are met by foreign competition, it is only natural for them to say "Foreign importations impede us in getting fair terms for our workmen; we must stop foreign importation." They do not, however, go as far as that, but the tendency is in that direction; and if that tendency had been united with the constant tendency of capitalist producers to try and get Protection for themselves, there is no knowing what mischief might have resulted. I think, however, that recent circumstances have shown that we had exaggerated the danger arising from this source. I think that I am justified by recent events in saying that the working men of England detest tyranny of all kinds, whether exercised by Capitalist producers or by Trades Union leaders; and when the latter at the Norwich Congress took upon themselves to propose resolutions contrary to the common sense of the country, and to the freedom of the employer and the workman, the Trades Union leaders suffered a great loss of importance and power. That is a great lesson to us to attach not too much importance to the temporary and extravagant opinions of Labour leaders.

There is another respect also in which the prospect is brighter —I mean the outcome of what is called "Fair Trade." So-called Fair Trade was at one time the subject of a serious agitation in this country, but I think that the danger has become less than it at one time threatened to be.

IMPERIAL AND COLONIAL DIFFERENTIAL DUTIES

But though the Fair Trade League has for some time ceased to make way in this country, there has in the colonies been a strong feeling that something might be done to bring about a closer union of the empire by imposing differential or protective duties.

THE OTTAWA CONFERENCE.

That feeling culminated in the proceedings of the Ottawa Conference, which passed a resolution urging the advisability of a customs arrangement between Great Britain and her colonies, by which trade within the empire might be placed on a more favourable footing than trade with foreign countries. At the same time in reading the report of those proceedings one cannot help being proud of the temper and tact and good sense with which they were conducted. The resolution to which I refer is as follows:

"The Conference records its belief in the advisability of a customs arrangement between Great Britain and her colonies, by which trade within the empire may be placed on a more favourable footing than that which is carried on with foreign countries."

"That until the mother country can see her way to enter into customs arrangements with her colonies it is desirable that, when empowered to do so, the colonies of Great Britain, or such of them as may be disposed to accede to this view, take steps to place each other's products, in whole or in part, on a more favourable customs basis than is accorded to the like products of foreign countries."

This resolution has been much discussed, and in the end, and as almost the last act of the late Government, Lord Ripon addressed two despatches to the colonies which I venture to think will prove an epoch in the history of this question. I do not think I ever remember to have read more exhaustive and more conclusive official documents than those two despatches. I believe they will settle the question. I do not believe that any future government will depart from them. And I am confirmed in that view by what I see Mr. Chamberlain said last night on a kindred

subject, viz., on Mr. Rhodes's proposal to introduce into the
dealings with Bechuanaland a provision that that country should
never impose higher duties on British goods than were now
imposed by the Cape Government. Now, Lord Ripon had refused
to have anything to do with that proposal because it was
unnecessary, and because it would have implied an opinion on the
part of the Imperial Government that it might be desirable to
impose differential duties in the colony on the goods of foreign
nations. Mr. Joseph Chamberlain, endorsing that view, said last
night that he saw no reason to depart from Lord Ripon's arrangements, and agreed that the clause was wholly unnecessary. The
despatches of Lord Ripon on the Resolution of the Ottawa
Conference seem to me so important that it is worth while to
state in precise terms the principles which, as it seems to me,
they lay down:—

PRINCIPLES OF COLONIAL TRADE ARRANGEMENTS.

1.—Freedom is greater than Free Trade. Great Britain does not
attempt to enforce her Free Trade policy on any self-governing colony.

2.—Great Britain will not abandon her own Free Trade policy for the
purpose of obtaining preferential treatment in her colonies.

3.—If, therefore, Imperial unity is to be strengthened by commercial
arrangements, those arrangements must be in the direction of Free Trade,
not of Protection, viz., by reduction of Protective duties in the colonies,
not by the imposition of differential duties in Great Britain.

4.—The self-governing colonies are at liberty to make commercial
arrangements with each other, provided they are consistent with Imperial
obligations, and with the interests of the rest of the empire.

5.—If a colony wishes to make special arrangements with a foreign
power it must be done through the Imperial Government.

6.—Such arrangements must be consistent with Imperial obligations
and with the interests of the rest of the empire.

7.—It is now a rule with the Imperial Government not to include the
colonies in any commercial arrangement with foreign countries without
their own consent. The case of the treaties with Belgium and Germany is
exceptional. But since the only thing which the colonies are prevented
from doing under these treaties is the grant of differential favours to Great
Britain; since Great Britain does not desire such favours; and since the
colonies would not grant such favours without reciprocal differential
favours which Great Britain is not prepared to grant; the exception is really
of no importance and would not justify a denunciation of the treaties.

These principles appear to me of the utmost importance, and to be
settled by Lord Ripon's despatches.

AGRICULTURE.

I turn from the more favourable side of the subject to what appear to me to be the possible dangers of the present, but I do not wish to exaggerate them. In the first place it is impossible to help feeling the greatest sympathy with the agricultural interest, which is suffering terribly. It is a favourable feature, nevertheless, that there is no expressed demand for Protection. Still, all sorts of remedies have been suggested, and one of them is a proposal to mark all foreign-made goods imported to this country with the name of the place of their manufacture. But as a remedial measure I believe this to be a pure delusion; because if a thing is good, people will buy it quite regardless of the home of its manufacture. As a matter of fact I am told that many cheap goods made in England are marked with French or German names, simply because people have got to believe that things cannot be had cheap unless they have been made in France or Germany. So far as this Club is concerned, the evil part of this suggestion is that it proposes to do this with respect only to foreign-made goods, and so invites the Custom House authorities to make a troublesome investigation for the purpose of seeing where the goods come from, and of stopping them if not properly marked. Here I say "Beware of the Custom House," and I say it with a tolerable knowledge of the tendency of the Customs in this direction. The Custom House has lost a great deal of its importance by the introduction of Free Trade measures, and it is but natural that its officials should seek to recover some part at least of their lost jurisdiction. But if you are thus to mark foreign goods, be consistent, and do the same with English-made goods; let us not have Stilton cheese which is not made at Stilton, or Southdown mutton which is not bred and nurtured on the Southdowns of Sussex! Do that, and our agriculturists will cease to press for the marking of foreign goods.

ALIEN IMMIGRATION.

Another danger that I see is the danger of interfering with alien immigration. This country has always been noted for its hospitality to foreign immigrants, and we owe a great deal of our prosperity to their industry and skill. Moreover, we probably send more emigrants to foreign countries than any other country in the world, so that we have much to lose in the way of retaliation if we try to stop foreign immigration. What was it that Lord Salisbury proposed? His alien Bill of 1894 proposed that the Board of

Trade inspector should have the power of prohibiting the landing of any alien "*who, in his opinion, was a pauper, or a person likely to become a public charge.*" Now I want to know how any Board of Trade inspector is to know whether a man who arrives in an English port, possibly with nothing in his pocket, is likely to become a charge on the public. It would be folly to prohibit a man from landing who is possibly bringing brains and muscles to the service of the community—and these are most useful to us no matter whence they come—simply because he has not five shillings in his pocket. I do not say there might not be cases in which we should require to take strong prohibitive measures, but no such emergency has yet arisen. Most of our immigrants are Jews, and it is well known that Jews take great care to provide for their own poor. The last Board of Trade returns—and they have been most carefully prepared—show that if this alien immigration is an evil, it is one that is not on the increase. Taking the whole number of the class who might possibly become destitute, it appears that as many of them leave us as come to us, and that on the whole the permanent number of persons belonging to this class is on the decrease rather than on the increase.

PRISON-MADE GOODS.

Another danger to which I shall refer—although the subject is not a large one—is one which arises out of the alleged importation to this country of prison-made goods. On February 19th there was a very curious debate on this subject in the House of Commons. On that occasion Colonel Howard Vincent moved the following resolution :—

"'That in the opinion of this House it is incumbent on Her Majesty's Government, in the interests of the industrial classes of the United Kingdom, at once to take steps to restrict the importation of goods made in foreign prisons by the forced labour of convicts and felons."

Colonel Howard Vincent carried that resolution through the House by a sort of triumphal procession. There was hardly a battle about it, and he had following in his train as humble satellites persons no less distinguished than Mr. Arthur Balfour and Mr. Joseph Chamberlain; while Ministers cowered on their bench, and did not dare to divide, and hardly ventured to remonstrate, when they might have done so on the broadest and largest grounds. That motion consisted of two premisses—a major and a minor. The first of them, the major premiss, was to the effect that if foreign prison-made goods can be imported so as to compete successfully with British goods, such freedom of importation is an evil. But that major premiss not only could not be proved but was as untrue as any of the dogmas of Protection. If you take into consideration the advantage from having English capital released for employment in more productive labour, the advantage of making goods to be sent abroad in payment for these prison-made goods, and the advantage to the consumer of cheaper goods, it is demonstrable that, as a matter of pure economy, the working classes of this country, and, indeed, the country at large, must gain instead of losing by their importation. But that major premiss was not even discussed, and Colonel Howard Vincent's motion was passed without a division. The Government, however, having accepted the resolution, did the best they then could. They appointed a Committee to consider the minor premiss—the question whether prison-made goods have successfully competed with English labour; and, if so, in what way it would be possible to stop the importation. The proceedings of that Committee are interesting. Colonel Howard Vincent produced some evidence, in itself weak, vague, and suspicious, and when he had done that Lord Thring and the rest of the Committee wanted to hear the other side. To this, however, Colonel Vincent and Colonel Bridgman would be no parties, and having heard all they wanted to hear, left the Committee. The rest of the Committee very properly went on. And what was the result? First of all they found that the only imported goods made in foreign prisons are brushes and mats, and these of a very poor sort. What did they find further? That these brushes and mats could be produced in those countries as cheaply by free labour as by prison labour, so that if prison-made brushes and mats were excluded the products of free labour would still compete with our own manufactures. It further appears from the evidence—most of which has been published in the newspapers—that there are manufacturers here who use machinery, and who compete successfully both with the foreigner and with English hand-made goods. They are not afraid of foreign goods, free or prison-made, and are, apparently, driving hand-made goods out of the market. It is the old story of the handloom weavers. It appears, moreover, that not only is our manufacture of brushes and mats not on the decrease, but actually on the increase, and that more persons are at present employed in the trade than before prison-made goods were imported to this country. And, lastly, it seems that we export to the countries from which prison-made goods come to us very nearly as much as we import. The minor premiss also is thus disproved, and the whole case fails. But the further question was asked, viz., What is it possible to do to restrict the importation of foreign prison-made goods? The answers given by the officials were very remarkable. The Customs authorities said that if a law were passed making it criminal to import prison-made goods there would not be the least chance of getting a conviction: no judge or jury would convict on such evidence as it would be possible to produce. But it might be possible to accomplish the object in view by means of an enlargement of the 42nd section of the Customs Act, a section which prohibits the importation of diseased cattle and obscene prints and things of that kind. If foreign prison-made goods were inserted in that section the Customs, by an exercise of official power, might stop them. But then came the further question, " How will you distinguish between foreign prison-made and foreign free-labour goods? " To this the answer is that the Customs cannot do it; and that the Government must pass an Order in Council placing under section 42 of the Customs Act all similar goods coming from suspected countries, whether prison-made or not, and that you must throw on persons who import the burden of proving that the goods are not prison-made. Can you conceive of tyranny greater than this? It would introduce all the mischievous and demoralising machinery of certificates of origin which our Free Trade system has enabled us to get rid of. But even that is not all, as any such measure would be an infringement of the Most Favoured Nation clause of our Commercial Treaties—the clause which is extremely important to us, and which it is our interest to have construed as liberally as possible. If, for instance, we were to say to Germany " We won't admit your brushes and mats," Germany would have the right to retort, " Why do you admit them from France? " I am fortified in this view by the very weighty opinion of Sir Robert Giffen. On the whole, if ever there was a rotten case for interfering by law with importation it is this. There has been much talk about the House of Lords, but I must say that the Lords have never been guilty of talking half as much nonsense as the House of Commons did on that 19th February. A strong point is made of the fact that hitherto we have checked the sale of goods made in our own prisons. But it so happens that in the report issued lately by the Commission on prisons and prison

B

labour a strong opinion is expressed that productive prison labour
ought to be encouraged. This opinion is supported by two
reasons—first, that it is better that prisoners should do something
towards their own maintenance; and second, that if we want to
treat these prisoners as men, if we have any hope of finally con-
verting them into useful members of society, instead of leaving
them to remain drones and plunderers, the best way is to teach
them to be useful. On the other hand labour on the crank and
treadmill is demoralising. On all these grounds it is quite clear
that to prohibit the sale of prison-made goods is wrong economi-
cally, socially, and morally. We may have a real sympathy with
the feelings of the working classes when they object to the competition of criminals whom they are themselves taxed to support.
But when examined carefully it is clear that the indulgence of
this feeling by prohibiting the sale of prison-made goods is wrong
and injurious to society and to the working classes themselves.

DUTY OF SPEAKING THE TRUTH.

It is, at any rate, our duty as members of this Club to speak
what we think to be the truth. I believe that politicians of all
kinds have been not only wrong but foolish in listening to the weak
demands of those who pretend to represent Labour. They will
suffer for it in the end, as we have seen in the case of Lord Salisbury
and the sugar bounties. The late Government, whether justly or
unjustly, are accused of having conceded too much to the demands
of the Trade Union leaders, and they suffered for this at the last
elections. And now I will conclude with mentioning what I have
often mentioned before, but which deserves to be repeated again
and again. The very last thing that John Bright ever said to me
was said after I had expressed some opinion favourable to our
new democratic constituencies. His reply was: "YES, THE PEOPLE
ON THE WHOLE ARE A VERY GOOD PEOPLE. THEY HAVE NOW GOT
THE POWER IN THEIR OWN HANDS; AND IF THOSE WHOSE BUSINESS IT
IS TO LEAD AND ADVISE THEM SPEAK THE TRUTH TO THEM, ALL WILL
GO WELL; BUT IF THEY DO NOT, GOD HELP THEM BOTH."

APOLOGIES FOR ABSENCE.

The CHAIRMAN called upon the Secretary to read the annual
report.

The SECRETARY (Mr. Richard Gowing), before reading the
report, said that many letters had been received from members, at
home and abroad, expressing their regret that they were prevented
from attending the meeting:—

The Right Hon. JOHN MORLEY wrote:—

I am just off to Scotland, and am sorry I shall not have returned in time for your meeting.

The Right Hon. HERBERT J. GLADSTONE, M.P., wrote:—

I am very sorry I cannot come on August 17th, as I expect to go north on the 16th at latest.

The Right Hon. Sir CHARLES DILKE, Bart., M.P., wrote:—

I should have been very glad to have attended the meeting on Saturday, the 17th, had I been in town, but I have a long-standing engagement to address the Lancashire miners at Ashton, near Wigan, on that day.

The Right Hon. A. H. D. ACLAND, M.P., wrote:—

I much regret that I am unable to be present on August 17th.

The Right Hon. Lord WELBY wrote:—

I regret to say that I shall not be in town to-morrow, and that I shall therefore be unable to attend the meeting of the Cobden Club, to be held at the National Liberal Club.

Sir PHILIP MANFIELD wrote:—

I regret I am unable to attend the meeting to-day in consequence of the appearance of my old enemy.

The Right Hon. GEORGE SHAW-LEFEVRE wrote:—

I regret that absence from London will prevent my being present at the meeting of the Cobden Club on Saturday next.

Mr. J. SHIRESS WILL, Q.C., M.P., wrote:—

I regret that absence from London will prevent my attendance at the meeting of the Cobden Club on the 17th.

Mr. A. C. HUMPHREYS-OWEN, M.P., wrote:—

I am sorry that I am prevented by another engagement from attending the meeting of the Cobden Club to-morrow. I found the Club leaflets and publications of great use in my election. I fear that very many farmers still believe that some sort of artificial enhancement of the price of agricultural produce is possible, and so long as this belief exists there is little hope of their considering any really practicable remedy for agricultural distress. The work of the Club, therefore, will be as necessary during the new Parliament as ever.

Baron MAX VON KUBECK (Austro-Hungarian Empire) wrote:

I am exceedingly sorry to state that even this year it is quite impossible for me to be present at the annual general meeting of the members of the Cobden Club, on account of many important private affairs keeping me at home during this summer. Please to accept my very best wishes for every success of the highly distinguished Club, to whose wise and beneficent tendencies I always do and shall adhere, with all my heart's convictions, and whose member to be I do and ever will feel most honoured. Please to convey my very sincerest regards to Mr. Thomas Bayley Potter.

Letters of regret were received also from the Right Hon. Sir W. V. Harcourt, M.P.; the Right Hon. H. H. Asquith, M.P.; the Right Hon. Lord Playfair; the Right Hon. the Marquess of Ripon; M. Yves Guyot (France), Signor Gaetano Tacconi (Italy), M. T. de Thoerner (Russia), M. Louis Strauss (Belgium), Mr. Simon Sterne (U.S. America), Mr. J. Fletcher Moulton, Q.C., Mr. J. A. Murray Macdonald, Mr. George Webb Medley, Mr. Joseph Robert Carter, etc. Within a few hours before the holding of this meeting a letter was received from Mr. A. Salaman, Hon. Secretary to the Free Trade League of Victoria, forwarding announcement of a vote of thanks of the Council of the League to the Cobden Club "for a recent generous gift of publications of the Club," and saying:—

The tariff of the colony is at present under discussion in the Legislative Assembly, and already a very great change in public sentiment is apparent. Hitherto tariff revision has meant increase of the Protective duties, but on the present occasion, so far as the items have been considered, reductions have been made. We have been obliged for the interesting leaflet on prison-goods, and if you could spare us a few copies for distribution we should be much obliged.

Mr. Edmund Bell, Auckland, New Zealand, wrote asking for leave to reprint for New Zealand circulation the Cobden Club pamphlet on "The Old Poor Law and New Socialism," as it is considered applicable to the state of things existing in New Zealand at the present time. Mr. Bell said:—

I have distributed thousands of copies of the Cobden Club publications throughout this country with, I believe, good effect. Free Trade doctrines are slowly but surely permeating the minds of the people, particularly the great body of producers, who are beginning to realise that while they have to sell in the cheapest markets they have to buy in the dearest, owing to the high tariff exactions. Nearly all the Club's leaflets have been distributed, so that a further supply will be acceptable.

Mr. Percy B. Wallace, assistant secretary to the London Society for the Extension of University Teaching, in announcing the name of the winner of the Cobden Club annual prize for the student who attains the first place in the economic classes of the society, said:—

I need not assure you what encouragement has been afforded to the students of economics by this generous offer of the Club during the past few years.

Mr. RICHARD GOWING, Secretary, then read the

REPORT OF THE COMMITTEE.

Your Committee were making preparations for convening the annual general meeting of members in the midsummer season as usual, when the recent political crisis and the resignation of Ministers, followed by the dissolution, seemed to render it desirable to postpone this meeting until the assembling of the new Parliament in August.

THE GENERAL ELECTION.

The general election has brought about a change in political affairs calculated to stimulate the Club to fresh vigilance in its work.

At our annual meeting seven years ago your Committee, in their report, observed that in the general election of 1886 a larger number of candidates professing Protectionist principles had been returned for borough and county constituencies than at any previous election since 1852. A period ensued during which Free Trade was challenged, in and out of Parliament, in various ways; and your Committee believe that this Club performed considerable public service, in combating the Protectionist resolutions of the National Union of Conservative Associations, the Sugar Bounties Countervailing Duties movement, the Marquess of Salisbury's extra-Parliamentary declaration in favour of a policy of fiscal retaliation, the proceedings of the United Empire Trade League, and of the since defunct Fair Trade League, and the Hofmeyr proposals for building up a wall of duties in Great Britain against imports from foreign countries for the purpose of giving an artificial preference to British colonial produce. The direct advocacy of Protectionist doctrines has been much less conspicious in the general election of 1895 than in that of 1886; but your Committee cannot conceal from themselves the fact that there are elements in the constitution of the new Parliament which seem to demand special watchfulness in the interests of Free Trade.

THE AGRICULTURAL DEPRESSION.

Remark was made, in the report presented at your last annual meeting, on the comparatively pacific current of fiscal events and developments during the preceding twelve months. The current has run a little less smoothly since then. Very naturally a good deal of consideration has been given, in and out of Parliament, to the serious depression in agriculture, and in the course of the discussion remedies have been suggested which would tend in the direction of a reversal of the long established fiscal policy of this country. Mr. Cobden was never wanting in regard for the interests of agriculture; nor has the Cobden Club ever been unmindful of those interests. During the last thirty years a large proportion of the Club's resources has been devoted to the effort to solve the problem of the profitable use and cultivation of the soil. But your Committee are convinced that nothing is so likely to hinder and defer the satisfactory and permanent solution of that problem as the re-opening, in any form or degree, of the question of relief from the prevalent troubles of agriculture in the shape of a revival of duties on imports of foreign or colonial agricultural or other produce.

FOREIGN PRISON-MADE GOODS.

When the question of legislation for the exclusion of cheap foreign prison-made brushes and other goods at our ports was brought recently before the House of Commons, your Committee felt that this was a question of principle which ought to be met by other arguments than those of the small magnitude of the importation and the practical difficulties of prohibition, and they were glad to publish a leaflet, kindly written by Lord Farrer, clearly and forcibly exposing the fallacy involved in any attempt to carry out the policy of exluding this class of merchandise from our markets. It was the sugar bounties question over again in another form ; and Lord Farrer demonstrated unanswerably that the free importation of these cheap articles from abroad, whatever their origin, is simply a matter of saving and gain, to the inhabitants of these islands, very largely exceeding any prejudicial consequences involved in any possible displacement of labour and capital, and carrying with it, in various industrial directions, quick and full reparation for any such loss by displacement. Every economist knows that the free importation of these brushes cannot be interfered with by Parliament without receding from the logic of the position on which our Free Trade system is based. But the folly of the movement, apart from the question of Free Trade, is likely to be demonstrated by the publication presently of the report of the Committee appointed to inquire into the question. This report is expected to show : that the competition from similar foreign articles made out of prison is at least as formidable as that of the prison-made goods; that machine-made brushes beat both alike ; that we export brushes largely; and that prison-made brushes cannot be excluded without recurring to the blunder of " certificates of origin " or endangering the " most-favoured-nation " treaties. It seemed to your Committee to be highly desirable to call attention to the strictly economic aspect of this question, as the Protectionist party, for the purpose of undermining the cause of Free Trade, were trading upon a sentiment, very excusable and easily evoked —the sentiment that honest men's labour was being supplanted by that of criminals.

THE MERCHANDISE MARKS ACT.

Your committee's attention has been called to the very injurious operation of the Merchandise Marks Act, in the case especially of goods from the United States to the continent of Europe which have been transhipped at British ports—at Hull, for example. The stamping of such goods with the place of origin is unnecessary as a condition of importation into the country of their destination, and irksome and in various ways objectionable to the manufacturers in the States ; but the absence of such marks has resulted in the confiscation of such goods under the Act by the customs authorities at Hull, and the action of those authorities has been upheld at headquarters. The consequences are irritating and mischievous to our commercial relations, and detrimental to our shipping and *entrepôt* trade, putting an end altogether, in some cases, to the transhipping of American cargoes at British ports ; and there is no countervailing advantage in any direction. Your Committee cannot regard this as a mere isolated misfortune arising out of an oversight in a section of the Act of Parliament. They are convinced that to a large extent the Merchandise Marks Act operates to the prejudice of international trade, with but little compensating advantage ; and they trust that at no very distant date Parliament will reconsider the whole question. The Cobden Club would be the last body to encourage fraudulent representations to the injury either of producers or consumers. But they cannot help feeling that the doctrine of marking goods with the name of their place of origin has been carried to excess ; that it is often a step which is of no value whatever to purchasers, while it lends itself readily to objectionable interference by the Customs with imported articles.

THE OTTAWA CONFERENCE.

The proceedings of the great Colonial Conference at Ottawa form an important section of an interesting chapter in the economics of commerce. The most essential points in the resolutions of the Conference, on the question of imperial trade, are contained in the following extracts :—

> The Conference records its belief in the advisability of a customs arrangement between Great Britain and her colonies, by which trade within the empire may be placed on a more favourable footing than that which is carried on with foreign countries.

> That until the mother country can see her way to enter into customs arrangements with her colonies it is desirable that, when empowered to do so, the colonies of Great Britain, or such of them as may be disposed to accede to this view, take steps to place each other's products, in whole or in part, on a more favourable customs basis than is accorded to the like products of foreign countries.

To carry out these purposes it was proposed to repeal legislation, and to cancel those provisions of certain British treaties with Belgium or Germany which have been made familiar, in the proceedings of the United Empire Trade League and otherwise, during several years. In a long despatch, dated June 28th last, addressed to the Governor-General of Canada, the Governors of the Australasian Colonies (except Western Australia), and the Governor of the Cape, the Marquess of Ripon, late Secretary of State for the Colonies, has, in reply to those resolutions, placed before the world a State paper which is one of the most valuable documents dealing with international fiscal relations to be found in the modern records of the Colonial Office. Lord Ripon sets forth at considerable length a series of the most complete and unanswerable reasons why, in the interest of Great Britain and the colonies and, indeed, in the best interests of the world's trade and of civilisation, the Ottawa

Conference Scheme cannot be carried out. So cogent and convincing is this document that your Committee cannot think that the distinguished Colonial statesmen who had these questions under consideration at Ottawa will any longer entertain the thought that the proposals contained in the resolutions in question are substantially either practicable or desirable. It has been a great gain, in the progress of the solution of the larger fiscal problems, that the public discussion of these questions should have resulted in this important decision of the Colonial Office. The outcome must make for advancement in the direction of Free Exchange, pure and simple, all over the world, as contrasted with the more or less delusive and disappointing operation of ingenious and elaborate fiscal schemes and treaties.

THE BRITISH EMPIRE LEAGUE.

Before the arrangements were made for the holding of the Ottawa Conference, the Central Organisation in London of the Imperial Federation League had been discontinued, apparently for the reason that its chief promoters in this country were not able to concur with the leading Canadian members in the scheme of discriminating duties between empire trade and foreign trade. Your Committee have observed, within the last few months, announcements of the formation of a new organisation called the British Empire League. The occurrence of the dissolution of Parliament probably deferred the development of the new League. Its object is " to maintain and strengthen the connection between the United Kingdom and the outlying portions of the empire by the discussion and promotion of questions of common interest, more particularly those relating to trade arrangements and mutual defence." Your Committee regard the conspicuous appearance of the names of Sir John Lubbock and the Duke of Devonshire, as leading promoters, as an assurance that the British Empire League will move upon lines consistent with the progress and development of free exchange throughout the world.

THE CECIL RHODES PROVISO.

Closely allied to the scheme of the Ottawa Conference was the proposed proviso of Mr. Cecil Rhodes in connection with clause 13 of the Matabeleland and Mashonaland agreement. Mr. Rhodes's proposal, as intended, would have led up, directly or indirectly, to a commercial union with South Africa on the basis of a tariff imposing higher duties on foreign · than on British goods. Lord Ripon's reasons why the Colonial Office should not concede the point, which appear in a Parliamentary Paper (House of Commons, 1894, No. 177), are on the same plane with the more recent despatch on the Ottawa Conference resolutions, referred to above. The real lesson of it all is: that taxes on imports, where necessary, should be for revenue only ; that they should not be in any way of a discriminating or Protective character, and that any attempt to make use of fiscal arrangements for the purpose of closer union between favoured countries is likely not only to be fiscally disadvantageous, but to defeat the objects it is intended to promote.

THE INDIAN COTTON DUTIES.

Your Committee, after serious consideration, took no part in the controversy on the question of the Indian Cotton Duties. By the policy of balancing the Indian import duties on cotton goods with countervailing excise duties in India, Sir Henry Fowler did his utmost to prevent the new duties from having a Protective operation. If those countervailing excise duties in practice do not effectually balance the customs duties, your Committee hope that measures may be taken for an equitable adjustment. The resources of statesmanship have not yet brought us within measurable distance of the time when the necessary public revenue can be raised without taxes on commodities, and until that time arrives the best that can be done is to take every precaution to prevent such duties from having a Protective incidence.

DISTRIBUTION OF PUBLICATIONS.

In the late general election your Committee took such measures as were practicable, in the emergency of the sudden dissolution of Parliament, to assist the masses of the electors to arrive at sound conclusions on the question of the continuance of our country's policy of the Freedom of Trade. Many thousands of leaflets and pamphlets were distributed, and a special leaflet was issued on " Economic Heresies " warning the working class electors especially against political and economic devices advocated for the purpose of artificially raising the prices of the necessaries of life and commodities of general consumption. The Cobden Club is in full sympathy with every movement having for its object improvements, by all legitimate means, in wages, the hours and conditions of labour, and the standard of living of the working population. Among the measures conducive to those ends are the freest possible operation of production, exchange, and distribution.

THE FREE TRADE QUESTION ABROAD.

Looking back upon the history of the tariff question abroad during the last fifteen or twenty years your Committee see no special cause for discouragement at the present time. From almost every quarter we hear of the failure of the Protective policy to produce satisfactory results in connection with the general interests of the population ; and every country has its able and active champions of Free Trade. The latest news from New South Wales is highly encouraging, and there are better tokens of Free Trade reaction in Victoria than have been seen for many years. Since the death of Mr. Cobden many experiments in Protection have been made in Europe, America, and the Southern Seas ; but everywhere it is being borne in upon the minds of statesmen and politicians that in Protection there is no finality. Through all these times of trial the Club has upheld the banner of Free Trade, and done its utmost to inspire confidence among the champions of Free Exchange, in the ultimate triumph of the principles of Richard Cobden.

MEDALS AND PRIZES.

The Cobden silver medal offered for competition in Political Economy at Bombay University for 1894 has been awarded to Mr. Nurjibhoy Hormasji

Wadia. In connection with the London Society for the Extension of University Teaching prizes of two guineas each have been awarded to Mr. Walter E. Ferguson and Mr. Walter H. Drew ; and a like prize has been awarded at the City of London College to Mr. G. W. Stonestreet. The prize of two guineas offered in connection with the lecture courses on Political Economy of the local examinations of the Cambridge and Oxford Universities have been made as follows:—Cambridge (1895), Miss Jennie Jackson, of the Hexham Centre ; Oxford (1894), Miss E. S. Brodrick, of the Cheltenham Centre ; (1895), Miss H. J. Strange, of Birmingham. The usual book prizes, to the value of £4, were awarded at Owens College, Manchester.

DEATHS.

The following is a list of the members of the Club whose death has been reported to the Committee since the last annual meeting : M. Gustave Adam (Paris), Mr. John Quincey Adams (U.S. America), M. A. Lalande (Bordeaux), H.R.H. the Comte de Paris, Dr. W. R. Smith (U.S. America), Senator Zebulon Vance (U.S. America), Mr. Geo. Wall (Colombo), Dr. Carl Braun (Leipzig), Herr Edward Ebertz (Berlin), Mr. Peter Esslemont, Comte Ferdinand de Lesseps, Lord Swansea, Lord Aberdare, and M. Léon Chotteau (France).

Special votes of regret were passed on the deaths of Mr. J. Quincey Adams and Mr. Geo. Wall.

NEW PUBLICATIONS.

Your Committee have in preparation new editions, specially edited and brought up to date, of the late Mr. A. Mongredien's "Free Trade and English Commerce," of which the Club has circulated 88,500 copies; and his "History of the Free Trade Movement in England," of which the Club has put in circulation about 10,000 copies.

The following publications have been added to the Club's stock for distribution since the last annual meeting :—

"Report of the Proceedings of the Annual Meeting of Members of the Cobden Club, 1894." 22,000 copies.

"Protection or Free Trade?" by Henry George. (Presented to the Club.) 500 copies.

Financial Reform Almanack. 13 copies.

"Free Trade v. Protection or Fair Trade." By Joseph Arch. (Curtis and Beamish, Coventry and Leamington.) 1,600 copies.

"Agricultural Distress : its Causes and its Remedies." By the Rt. Hon. C. Seale-Hayne, M.P. (*Daily Western Times* Office.) 10,000 copies.

Total number of books, pamphlets, &c. (exclusive of leaflets), added to the Club's stock since last Annual Meeting, 34,119.

The following new leaflets have been printed :—

103.—"What Shall we Do with Foreign Brushes?" By the Rt. Hon. Lord Farrer. 50,000 copies.

104.—"To the Electors of the United Kingdom. On Economic Heresies." 10,000 copies.

Cobden Club Leaflets translated into Welsh, reprinted, Nos. 3, 4, 5, and 7. 10,000 copies each.

MR. J. W. PROBYN.

Mr. J. W. PROBYN, in moving the adoption of the report, said: Mr. Potter and gentlemen, after the extremely able and exhaustive speech of Lord Farrer I feel there is little left for me to say. I entirely concur with everything that has fallen from his lips, and we cannot do better than cause the speech to which he has treated us to be printed and circulated. It seems to me that we need in no way be discouraged by the present state of things, which to my mind is strong proof of the soundness of the basis on which our system rests. No doubt those who have particular interests to develop would wish to tamper with that principle for their special benefit, and it is our duty to watch the proceedings of those who might be so interested—to see that they do not undermine the great principle on which our whole fiscal policy rests. This tampering for the benefit of special interests is being done in various ways, and latterly the very clever plan has been adopted of trying to enlist our philanthropic sympathies while attacking what our opponents call our economic "fallacies." Lord Farrer has already dealt with the question of prison-made brushes and mats, exposing the fallacy on which the whole of that attack rested. Now I should like to tell you about a little experience of my own. A few days after the general election I met a farmer in my neighbourhood, the best of Conservatives and a good Protectionist at heart. I said to him "Well, now you will be looking forward to at least a 5s. or 10s. duty on foreign corn?" He said "Oh, no, we cannot lay an embargo on the food of the people." I said "I am glad to hear you say so." Indeed, I felt somewhat encouraged that a farmer, full of Conservatism, had given up the erroneous notion of bolstering up English corn by putting a duty on foreign corn. Then I said to him "How are your friends going to treat you? If they are not going to put a duty on foreign corn, do they propose to put heavy duties on agricultural machinery and other manufactured goods?" No, he did not think that that would be done. So that altogether it seemed to me that the prospect was brighter than I had anticipated. There was no prospect, according to him, of a tax on foreign corn or agricultural machinery. This is a small fact, but I think we may gain encouragement from it as a sign of the direction in which the current is flowing. In our colonies we may see, as a result of the Ottawa conference, that there is a great doubt coming over the minds of our friends who were formerly in favour of a sort of imperial colonial customs league, because the colonies are anxious to protect themselves against one another. We, of course, offer them a simple remedy. We say "Your union with us will be perfect if you will follow our advice and become Free Traders as we are." New South Wales has tried a little Protection and is giving it up. The great truth is coming to be recognised that a tax for revenue purposes does no harm, but that tariffs imposed for the purpose of protecting special interests are necessarily the enemies of free and fair competition. I have great pleasure in moving the adoption of the report.

MR. I. S. LEADAM.

Mr. I. S. Leadam, in seconding the motion, said: Mr. Potter and gentlemen, I confess I cannot share the sanguine opinion entertained by Mr. Probyn as to the condition of the new Parliament. I cannot help remembering the Oxford Conference of Conservatives held a few years ago at which resolutions in favour of a return to Protection were carried by an overwhelming majority. I was opposed recently by a gentleman who, in his address, stated that he was a believer in Free Trade, but that he desired to see tariffs put upon foreign importations with the object of placing our workmen on the same footing as foreigners. It is difficult to say whether that address was adroitly framed with the object of catching the votes of Free Traders as well as Protectionists, or whether it was an example of the infantine ignorance which afflicts some of our legislators. I am inclined to suspect that it was a case of infantine ignorance, and am reminded of the Swedish Chancellor Oxenstiern's commentary: "You see, my son, with how little wisdom this world is governed." There is a class of persons who say that they are thoroughly in favour of Free Trade, but are beginning to doubt whether its conclusions ought not to be modified by other considerations in practice, and whether the theory should not conform to new conditions of the present. These people do not appear to reflect that the theory of Free Trade is not simply à priori, but one which has been built up, as logicians say, by "induction from particulars," and which has been founded on actual experience. The only remedy one can apply to such a state of mind is the study of history. One can only ask these gentlemen to re-acquaint themselves with the condition of things which existed when the Free Trade system was adopted, and when Peel inculcated the maxim that the only way to fight hostile tariffs is by free imports. There is another reason why I think Mr. Probyn entertains too sanguine a view of the political situation. Undoubtedly the rank and file of the Conservative party have denounced Sir William Harcourt's budget and pledged themselves against it. But if Sir William Harcourt's budget is to be repealed it will be necessary to procure funds to carry on the business of the country from some other sources than at present, and it will at once suggest itself to the minds of those who are committed to Protection to revive some of the schemes to which Lord Farrer has alluded. An obvious source of supply would be the re-introduction of a Bill for taxing sugar, as was proposed by the Conservative Government in 1889, which proposal was happily defeated through the agency of the Cobden Club. We must not make the mistake of believing that our difficulties are over. For my own part I think that the indications, so far as the Conservatives are concerned, are by no means wholly favourable; and therefore it is necessary that the Club should maintain its full complement of members, so as to be in a position to protect a Ministry we will presume to be favourably disposed towards Free Trade against the assaults of their own misguided followers.

MR. GEORGE COLE (CANTERBURY).

Mr. George Cole said: Mr. Potter, ladies and gentlemen, I rise not merely for the purpose of supporting the motion, but also for the purpose of assuring you that your leaflets and other publications are highly appreciated by those electors with whom I come in contact. I believe that your pamphlets, &c., produce good results if judiciously and carefully distributed in quiet times; but on the other hand I do not think they do much good if the distribution is delayed until the excitement occurs which generally arises within ten days of a parliamentary election. In the presence of the talented men and clever writers whom I see before me I will not venture to praise or criticise the publications themselves, but I think it well to say a few words upon the difficulties with which the distributors of them have to contend. I am one of your volunteer unpaid distributors, who has the privilege of coming face to face with the ordinary average elector: the small farmer, the retail shopkeeper, the working tradesman, and the mechanic, who do not generally read a daily newspaper; and I can assure you that your pamphlets are fully appreciated by them. I took an active part in Sir Israel Hart's successful campaign at Hythe and Folkestone last month (as well as assisting in two other constituencies), and I wish to say that if your leaflets had been widely and judiciously distributed three months before the last general election you would have had a much more satisfactory result at a small expenditure of money than you have now to record. It is an unfortunate fact that the average elector knows very little about the political history of his own country extending over the last sixty years, and therefore, for your pamphlets to be properly read and to be thoroughly effective they should be widely distributed several months before an election. Now having praised your publications and thanked you for your work I wonder if you will allow me to point out where we and the publications fail. It is venturesome of me to criticise, but it occurs to me to say that there is a section of the people, and an educated section, whom your literature entirely fails to reach—I mean boys of between 12 and 16 who are just about to leave the elementary and intermediate schools. Upon enquiry you will find that the junior masters, as well as the scholars, know very little of the political history of their country for the last fifty years; and when we attempt to reach them by sending your literature we find that scholars aged about 14 years have not time to study the recent history of their own country! The fact is that the Civil Service and Cambridge Local Examiners do not put their questions on English history on any period of recent date. Consequently headmasters, finding that recent knowledge does not pay, put their scholars to study history of, say, the period of William I. instead of William IV., or of Richard I. instead of Victoria. The scholars know very little about what has happened since the great Reform of 1832-35; and consequently when these young lads first become voters they have everything to learn in a few weeks, and are very easily misled. The remedy I suggest is that the Cobden Club, and you, gentlemen, individually, should strongly urge the Cambridge Local Examiners, and other similar examiners, to bring their questions on English history down to quite recent times. If you can influence the official examiners, the schoolmasters will soon follow their lead. The schoolmasters will be pleased to teach the " History of our own times," but at present they have no inducement to do so; and consequently you have, growing up, a generation which knows absolutely nothing of the period of high tariffs, and the misery which resulted from so-called "Protective duties." Unless you get these lads to learn recent history the Cobden Club of ten years hence will have all its educational work to do over again, when the old men who remember the period of high tariffs have died out. In the meantime, the Cobden Club must not fail to strengthen the hands of the Chairman, so that there may still be continued the free distribution of your excellent literature.

MR. THOMAS HANBURY.

Mr. THOMAS HANBURY said: Mr. Potter and gentlemen, I had the honour of addressing the annual meeting last year, calling attention to the enormous appreciation of gold as a question of vast economic importance worthy of receiving the close attention of this Club. The year that has since passed has only served to make apparent that no feasible remedy except bimetallism has been proposed for the admitted evils I then described. The resolution of Mr. R. L. Everitt, member for the Woodbridge division of Suffolk, accepted by the late Liberal Government and unanimously passed by the House of Commons on February 26th last, only serves to emphasise this, while in the recent elections the question of bi-metallism *versus* gold-metallism rose superior to politics, and in some instances a declaration inimical to bimetallism caused the rejection of the candidate. At the last annual meeting, sir, you announced that the Committee, after much consideration, had decided that it was better for the Cobden Club not to meddle with the question of bimetallism, but I believe it is an open secret that this matter has again been under deliberation, and that some members of the Committee desire that the Club should espouse the cause of gold-monometallism, attacking in leaflets or othewise the cause of bimetallism, which has the sympathy, as I think, of a majority of those of our countrymen who have paid any attention to the subject. Without, therefore, wishing to initiate a discussion on bimetallism, I claim the right to adduce a few weighty reasons why such a course of action should be antagonistic to the ideas of some of the most honoured members of the Club, and directly at variance with the principles of Free Trade, which I hold should be maintained with the utmost robustness by the followers of

Cobden. The Bimetallic League may, without exaggeration, be called the off-spring of the Cobden Club, for M. Cernuschi, the father of bimetallism, and who invented the word, is a member of the Club. Gentlemen, our worthy Chairman on a memorable occasion, with that modesty which is so characteristic of him, pointed to the late Sir Louis Malet as the intellectual head of the Cobden Club. Sir Louis Malet was no less esteemed by the bimetallists as one of the founders of their league. The name of Bright is an honoured one in the Cobden Club, and in the person of the Right Hon. Jacob Bright we have at once a member of their Committee and a vice-president of the Bimetallic League, and the same remark applies to Mr. Provand, M.P. After recent utterances I should be rash in claiming Lord Farrer as a bimetallist, but there can be no doubt that he and the other eminent gentlemen who signed the report of the Royal Commission on gold and silver, 1888, have furnished the Bimetallic League with its strongest arguments in such passages as these:—

Sec. 115.—"The remedy which has been put before us most prominently and as most likely to remedy the evils complained of to the fullest extent possible, is that known as bimetallism.

"So long as that system was in force we think that, notwithstanding the changes in the production and the use of the precious metals, it kept the market price of silver approximately steady at the ratio fixed by law between them, namely 15½ to 1.

Sec. 107.—"We think that in any conditions fairly to be contemplated in the future, so far as we can forecast them from the experience of the past, a stable ratio might be maintained if the nations we have alluded to were to accept and strictly adhere to bimetallism, at the suggested ratio. We think that if in all these countries gold and silver could be freely coined, and thus become exchangeable against commodities at the fixed ratio, the market value of silver as measured by gold would conform to that ratio, and not vary to any material extent.

Sec. 119.—"Apprehensions have been expressed that if a bimetallic system were adopted gold would gradually disappear from circulation. If, however, the arrangement included all the principal commercial nations, we do not think there would be any serious danger of such a result."

As these important conclusions, only arrived at after a most laborious and exhaustive examination of the whole question, extending over a period of two years, are apt to be forgotten, I have had extracts from the report bearing on the subject of bimetallism reprinted for distribution; they form what has been aptly called the Magna Charta of the bimetallists. I am quite aware that the hesitancy of certain members of the Club is the fear that bimetallists really aim at unduly enhancing the necessaries of life, and that, therefore, it is the duty of the Club to withstand whatever is prejudicial to the working classes, but surely in such a matter the represenatives of labour are no bad judges, and I hold in my hand a list of thirty-eight labour organisations throughout the country who are in full sympathy with bimetallism, the list being headed by the United Textile Factory Workers, who have given £500 to the funds of the Bimetallic League. A year ago I argued with the rupee (a token coin) in my hand; since then it has continued to be sold in London to the extent of six millions of rupees per week, and at the average price of 13d., though it contains more silver than our two shilling piece. To-day I ask leave to exhibit the new British dollar, containing 374½ grains of pure silver, now being minted in Bombay for use in China, the Straits, and elsewhere. It is probably destined to play a tremendous part in the transference of English industries to Asiatics, since it only costs about 2s. and is good for the purchasing of 4s. worth of labour in the East. It may be called the coin which best exemplifies free trade in silver. Place it alongside our florin as emblem of Protection, containing 161 grains of pure silver, and you will easily perceive how impossible it is to convince English working men that they are getting fair play while their competitors are thus receiving double money. Why, then, is one coin so big and the other so small as only to contain ten pennyworth of silver? Gold monometallists will tell you it is "the luck of the situation," but the real reason is that they insist on strong Protection for gold, fearing that the enormous appreciation they are now enjoying without having earned it might disappear if the toiling millions were allowed to have free silver money, a duty of 125 per cent. being now levied upon it under the name of seigniorage before it is allowed to reach the pockets of the people. The gold protectionist, enthroned in Lombard-street on his vast store of gold, and gloating over such an appreciation of his gilt-edged securities as the world has never seen, cries to those who live by industry, "It is all a mistake, there is no lack of gold, only we require you to produce double the quantity of commodities for the same money as was paid you twenty years ago." The toiling millions reply, "The task is impossible, especially as we perceive our formidable competitors in Asia are to be supplied with British silver money on Free Trade principles, while we are groaning under the curse of Protection." Can it be doubted for a moment on which side the sympathies of the Cobden Club should lie, since it is the old, old story of Protection *versus* Free Trade, disguise it how you may? In corroboration of this view I will quote the late Professor Emile de Laveleye, whose splendid services to the cause of Free Trade on the Continent are known to every Free Trader, and who was one of the staunchest bimetallists. In an article in the *Pall Mall Gazette* he wrote:—"It remains to be seen how long England will go on maintaining the unjust monopoly of gold, so rendering impossible the realisation of Cobden's beautiful motto— 'Peace, Goodwill, and Free Trade amongst men.' Let us hope that the future leaders of the English democracy will see that the iniquitous monopoly accorded to gold sacrifices the most active part of the nation to the idle part, and that they will restore to the two precious metals the *rôle* which science, history, commerce, and the free consent of the peoples had guaranteed them throughout the past."

MR. PROVAND, M.P.

Mr. PROVAND said: Mr. Potter and gentlemen, as my name has been mentioned by the last speaker I may be excused for wishing to say a few words on the subject dealt with by him, which if it is not that of bimetallism is at least the question of gold and silver; and it matters not whether it is taken up on the side of gold or of silver, this Club, if it embarks upon it, will very soon come to be a thing of the past. Once let it meddle with this subject and the Club will not survive three months. Mr. Hanbury has spoken on the side of silver, but a gold monometallist will say, if this Club supports the case for silver, that it is advocating the protection of that metal. The objects of the Cobden Club are purely fiscal, and with these alone should it be concerned. You may find a man to contend that the bimetallic question is a fiscal question, but my view is that to treat it as such would be to depart from the original object and intention for which the Club exists. Mr. Hanbury has told us how he considers that question affected the result of the late elections, but again I say that that is no reason why it should be included in the deliberations of this

Club. My advice to the Club is: Do not meddle with subjects entirely outside the scope of the Club. There is plenty of work for us to do without touching the gold and silver question. Mention has been made of the new House, but as far as I have been able to gather, there is nothing to fear from the present Parliament. I have spoken on the subject with two of the new members. One of them, who represents a division south of London, told me that his constituents were largely Protectionists. The other, who represents a division west of London, said the same thing; while a West of England member said that although a large number of his constituents were anxious for Protection, it would be folly to grant it. As a proof of this he said that they had been able to buy foreign barley for feeding at an unusually low figure, and that would have been impossible with Protection. I would draw your attention to a very important letter which appeared in the *Times* of August 3rd, written by the member for North-East Bethnal Green, in which he drew attention to what had taken place in the seventeen eastern divisions at the last general election. He mentioned that there had been a large number of leaflets distributed in those divisions by the British Industries, Trade and Labour Defence League. The secretary of that League is Mr. J. P. Ewing, and no doubt we should be able to get copies of them on application. The object of the literature distributed was to show that the present fiscal arrangements of this country enabled foreign governments to put large duties on manufactured goods, and so shut out British manufactures. The writer went on to point out that this had the effect of paralysing the labour and lowering the wages of British artisans. I am sure that there was not a statement in that leaflet the falsehood of which has not been proved time and again. I think the Club should turn its attention to distributing its own leaflets in that part of London. How strongly the minds of men are infected with the notion of Protection is seen in that letter to the *Times* to which I have referred. Herein, I think, is ample scope to occupy the time of this Club and its money; but take up the question of gold and silver, and our Club would die a natural death in a year. I think some one of the gentlemen congratulated himself on the outlook in foreign countries. The United States have undoubtedly come to see the advantages of the lower tariff of the Wilson kind over the higher rates of the Mc.Kinley, but that was not before prosperity had begun to come. Only two months ago I was there, and can say that the feeling in favour of a lower tariff was growing, although a few months before that no one was in favour of anything but Protection up to the hilt. Mr. Probyn has referred to the experiments in Protection in New South Wales. New South Wales adopted Protection quite recently; but still more recently Mr. Reid went to the country on the question of Free Trade *versus* Protection, and the country decided in favour of taxation for revenue purposes, but not for protecting industries. I hope the attention of this Club will be strictly confined to those objects for which it was founded.

Mr. POTTER: With reference to the subject treated of by Mr. Hanbury I wish to say that Mr. Hanbury was anxious to lay his case before the Club, and he has done so very clearly; but the Committee has decided not to touch bimetallism, as it would merely lead to differences.

MR. SOPER.

Mr. SOPER agreed that the Club should have nothing to do with the question of bimetallism. The report said, however, that the Club should be ready to assist and sympathise with any cause tending to promote the welfare of our industrial classes. Now, they had an immense number of unemployed in the country, whose only hope of subsistence was out of the land. The land, however, was under the control of private individuals, and therefore was for that purpose inaccessible. He thought, however, that it could be made conisstent with the objects of the Club to bring the land under the direct control of the nation. He was quite sure that Cobden, had he been living, would have seen the necessity of this course. The question of the nationalisation of the land was very much to the front now, and was becoming more pressing every day.

Mr. POTTER: I am afraid we cannot undertake more than we have on our hands.

MONS. EDOUARD SEVE.

Mons. EDOUARD SEVE said that his friend, Emile de Laveleye, had done his best to introduce the question of bimetallism before the Cobden Club twenty years ago, but had failed. The question was a difficult and dangerous one, and had better be left alone by the Club, which had already quite enough to do.

MR. THOMAS LOUGH, M.P.

Mr. THOMAS LOUGH, M.P., said with regard to the Club's position towards bimetallism that there had been a league formed in the city of London, with the advantage of having plenty of money at its back. It was called the Gold Standard Defence Association, and it was doing its work admirably; so that it was not necessary that the Cobden Club should take up the currency question. He thought, however, that the Club should do more than it had done in the way of publications.

Mr. POTTER: It is a question of funds.

Mr. LOUGH, continuing, said he noticed that the Cobden Club had a large balance in hand, which might well be spent in preparing and issuing leaflets. The late election had been won on the question of "Fair" Trade. True, they had Local Veto and other things; but in the metropolis nothing did more to injure the cause of the late Government than the misrepresentations which were made about foreign brushes and mats. He had written to the Secretary of this Club, enclosing the very letter published in the *Times* of which Mr. Provand had spoken; and to that gentleman's narrative he wished to add that in seventeen East End constituencies there were 50,000 members of the British Industries, Trade and Labour Defence League said to be enrolled in the few months before the election, and they argued that they won fourteen out of the seventeen constituencies by this advocacy of Protection alone. He thought some reply should be made to that letter and those leaflets, and the attention of every unfortunate candidate and member of Parliament should be devoted to combating the views it contained. Employers represented everywhere that there could not be prosperity under a Liberal Government. If the Cobden Club did good work funds would be sure to come in. As far as he knew, in the course of last year 20,000,000 pamphlets were issued on the Liberal side, and 25,000,000 on the Tory side.

Mr. POTTER: We had not the money.

Mr. LOUGH: Money is not a requisite at all. If you write a good leaflet the money will come in. If we get a good economist to draw up these leaflets means will be found to circulate them. I believe that the whole question of Free Trade has arisen in all its magnitude, and we should do something to justify our existence.

Mr. POTTER: The proposition is a very good one if it could be carried out. We began the system of leaflets 15 or 20 years ago, when the agricultural labourer was first enfranchised. But our funds have never been equal to the demand. Whenever we get a good leaflet we publish it.

Mr. LOUGH: You appear to have to your credit £500, and for that sum you could issue 5,000,000 leaflets.

Mr. POTTER: We will take the matter into consideration as far as our means will allow.

MR. THOMAS HANBURY.

Mr. THOMAS HANBURY was satisfied with the decision that had been arrived at by the meeting on the subject of bimetallism, because he saw he was in a hopeless minority. If, however, members would read his speech again they would see that he was arguing that the Club should not distribute leaflets in aid of the monometallists. He accepted the situation frankly that it was not the duty of the Club to meddle with the question of bimetallism. While he held that silver was a commodity, and had no right to be taxed to the enormous extent that was being done, he bowed to the decision of the majority that the Club should not discuss the question.

The Report was adopted.

MR. MARTIN WOOD.

Mr. MARTIN WOOD, in moving the re-election of the Committee, said he did so with much pleasure, seeing that its members included men of talent and capacity to fulfil all the objects of the Club. But there was one of its objects that had been somewhat lost sight of in recent years. He referred to an important portion of the Club's motto: "Peace and Goodwill." The founders of the Club would, he thought, have more directly combated the recent ruinous increase in naval and military expenditure. Such insistance would promote Free Trade itself, for he thought the high tariffs on the Continent were directly traceable to the maintenance of bloated armaments, which represented an enormous non-productive consumption. These had helped in the last twenty years to add something like forty or fifty millions to the expenditure of Europe. If only that money could be set back what would the effect be on trade? Why, trade would go up by leaps and bounds! He would challenge disproof of the proposition that this enormous waste of resources, more than all other causes put together, explains such depression of commerce and industry as at present exists. Hence he trusted the Club would attack this great obstacle to the adoption of its principles.

MR. G. J. HOLYOAKE.

Mr. G. J. HOLYOAKE, in seconding, said there was nothing in the changed political attitude of the industrial classes to discourage anybody. Persons supposed it was a new manifestation of ingratitude on the part of the working class that they had returned a Conservative House of Commons. But he had seen the same thing done over and over again by gentlemen. A few years ago, when Mr. Gladstone was forced to resign, an eminent Radical wrote his belief that it would be better to have Disraeli in power. He was under the impression that Disraeli would give the people something which Mr. Gladstone had refused, and he argued that Mr. Gladstone, excluded from office for a couple of years, would come back reinvigorated by their ingratitude. At the last election specious promises were made to men who ought to have had the sense to know better than that they would be redeemed. The result, however, was not likely to endanger progress.

The motion was carried unanimously.

THE COMMITTEE.

The following gentlemen form the Committee:—The Right Hon. Arthur H. Dyke Acland, M.P., Mr. Thomas Gair Ashton, M.P., Mr. William Birkmyre, the Right Hon. Jacob Bright, Mr. Alexander H. Brown, M.P., Mr. Dadabhai Naoroji, the Right Hon. Sir C. W. Dilke, Bart., M.P., Lord Farrer, Mr. Richard C. Fisher, Mr. William Fowler, the Right Hon. Herbert J. Gladstone, M.P., Mr. Alfred Illingworth, Sir Wilfrid Lawson, Bart., M.P., Mr. I. S. Leadam, Mr. E. A. Leatham, the Right Hon. Sir John Lubbock, Bart., M.P., Mr. J. A. Murray Macdonald, Mr. William Mather, Mr. George Webb Medley, Mr. J. Fletcher Moulton, Q.C., Lord Northbourne, Mr. A. C. Humphreys-Owen, M.P., Mr. J. Allanson Picton, Lord Playfair, Mr. T. Bayley Potter (hon. sec.), Mr. J. W. Probyn (hon. treasurer), Mr. Andrew D. Provand, M.P., Mr. C. S. Salmon, Right Hon. Charles Seale-Hayne, M.P., Mr. J. P. Thomasson, Mr. T. Fisher Unwin, Sir William Wedderburn, Bart., M.P., and Lord Welby.

SIR WILFRID LAWSON.

Sir WILFRID LAWSON, in moving a vote of thanks to the chairman, said that they had faith in their principles, and they were as cheerful and as hopeful as ever they had been. They were as steadfast in their principles as the girl who, while on her way to India, wrote home to the bishop's wife to say:—" We are going down the Red Sea in tremendous heat, but still I am a member of the Church of England." (Laughter.) They held on to their principles; and this reminded him of some words he had read years ago in the *Saturday Review*:—" Nothing is so certain as the ultimate triumph of those who know." And they knew that their principles were right, and would some day or other triumph. The Cobden Club believed in the freedom of exchange ; that was the basis on which it was founded, and to fetter any man in the power of exchanging with his neighbour was merely a branch of slavery. The bulk of the farmers in this country had an idea that the Tory party was somehow in favour of Protection, and would do something for them at some time or other. That was one of the main reasons why a Tory majority was returned to Parliament. But this great Government which was going to set the agricultural labourer on his legs was already beginning to flounder about in a most extraordinary manner. The subject of agricultural depression was before the House on Friday night, but what satisfaction did they get from the Government ? Nothing but a lot of vague, indefinite, and incomprehensible promises and empty protestations. As for himself, as he sat listening to the wonderful speeches that night, he thought he heard a still small voice from the tomb. It was the voice of Disraeli, and he heard him say " A Conservative Government is an organised hypocrisy." It was for them to do what they could to get rid of this sham. The world was divided into two classes—people who constructed shams and those who overthrew them, and the Cobden Club was doing good work in identifying itself with the latter. Let it be their boast to speak always boldly—not like the Irish member who said, " I am not going to stand again, therefore I will speak the truth." (Laughter.) Let it be the steadfast purpose of the Cobden Club to go on speaking the truth, writing the truth, and acting the truth, for " the truth shall make us free." He hoped the chairman would live to see the triumph of those principles for which he had done so much.

MR. A. D. PROVAND, M.P.

Mr. PROVAND, M.P., seconded the motion. In doing so he asked the meeting to excuse him for alluding to a remark which had fallen from Mr. Martin Wood. That gentleman had said that one reason of commercial depression in Europe was the unproductive investment of enormous capital in "bloated armaments." But the first question to be asked was: What is a "bloated armament?" He himself was a believer in the necessity of a large navy, larger and more powerful even than was our navy at the present time. It was no secret that this necessity was created by the attitude of France. Personally, he liked and respected the French people, but if anyone wished to know the feeling of French journalists and politicians towards us he referred him to a recent number of the *National Review*. Whilst there was no people for whom as a whole he had greater respect and admiration, his opinion of some French journalists and politicians was one he preferred not to express. He warned the Club to take up with no questions outside its original purpose, as to do that would assuredly produce a disintegrating effect.

MONS. EDOUARD SEVE.

Mons. EDOUARD SEVE supported the resolution, and hoped that the Chairman would be spared for many years to continue at the head of the Cobden Club.

MR. T. B. POTTER.

Mr. T. B. POTTER said: It is now nearly thirty years since the Cobden Club was started. I went into the House of Commons in 1865, and in the early spring of 1866 it was suggested to me, and I undertook the task of forming this Club. Since then I hope we have done some good. We have not done all that we might have done, but we have done as much as we could. I thank you very much. (Applause.)

The meeting then separated.

WORKS PUBLISHED for the COBDEN CLUB

By Cassell & Company, Limited, La Belle Sauvage, London, E.C.

A Study of Small Holdings. By W. E. BEAR. Price *6d.*

Retaliation and Commercial Federation. By the Rt. Hon. Lord FARRER. Price *3d.*

Industrial Freedom. By B. R. WISE. Price *5s.*

Wages and Hours of Labour. By the Rt. Hon. Lord PLAYFAIR, K.C.B. Price *3d.*

Tenancy and Ownership. By JOHN WATSON, M.A. Price *1s.*

Presentation of an Address to Mr. T. B. Potter, M.P. Price *3d.*

The Sugar Convention. By the Rt. Hon. Lord FARRER. Price *1s.*

The Sugar Convention and Bill. By the Rt. Hon. Lord FARRER. Price *6d.*

What Protection does for the Farmer and Labourer. By I. S. LEADAM, M.A. *Fifth Edition.* Price *1s.*

Local Government and Taxation in the United Kingdom. With Contributions by the Hon. G. C. BRODRICK, C. T. D. ACLAND, M.P., LORD EDMOND FITZMAURICE, &c. Edited by J. W. PROBYN. Cloth, *5s.*

Free Trade *versus* Fair Trade. *New Edition.* By the Rt. Hon. Lord FARRER. Price *5s.*

Free Trade and English Commerce. By AUGUSTUS MONGREDIEN. Price *6d.*

Pleas for Protection Examined. By AUGUSTUS MONGREDIEN. *6d.*

Popular Fallacies regarding Trade and Foreign Duties: Being the "SOPHISMES ÉCONOMIQUES" of FRÉDÉRIC BASTIAT. Adapted to the Present Time by Sir E. R. PEARCE EDGCUMBE. *4th Edition, Revised. 6d.*

Western Farmer of America. By AUGUSTUS MONGREDIEN. *3d.*

The Transfer of Land by Registration under the Duplicate Method operative in British Colonies. By Sir ROBERT TORRENS, K.C.M.G. Price *6d.*

Transfer of Land by Registration of Title. By T. R. COLQUHOUN DILL, B.A. Price *6d.*

The Secretary of State for India in Council. By WM. BIRKMYRE, M.P. Price *6d.*

The A B C of Free Trade. By E. N. BUXTON. *New and Revised Edition.* Price *3d.*

The Caribbean Confederation. By C. S. SALMON. *1s. 6d.*

Cottage Gardens and Fruit Culture. By the Right Hon. W. E GLADSTONE, M.P. Price *1d.*

The Grain Tax in Ceylon. By C. S. SALMON. Price *3d.*

The Tariffs of the United States. By the Rt. Hon. Lord PLAYFAIR, K.C.B. Price *3d.*

CASSELL & COMPANY, Limited, Ludgate Hill, London.